W9-CCD-936

BUILD YOUR BUSINESS

START YOUR BABYSITTING BUSINESS

by Melissa Higgins

CAPSTONE PRESS
a capstone imprint

Snap Books are published by Capstone Press
1710 Roe Crest Drive, North Mankato, Minnesota 56003
www.mycapstone.com

Library of Congress Cataloging-in-Publication Data

Names: Higgins, Melissa, 1953- author.
Title: Start your babysitting business / by Melissa Higgins.
Description: North Mankato, Minnesota : Capstone Press, [2018] | Series: Snap
    books. Build your business | Includes bibliographical references and index.
Identifiers: LCCN 2016047902| ISBN 9781515766919 (library binding) | ISBN
    9781515767039 (ebook (pdf)
Subjects: LCSH: Babysitting—Juvenile literature. | Child care
    services—Juvenile literature.
Classification: LCC HQ769.5 .H543 2018 | DDC 649/.10248—dc23
LC record available at https://lccn.loc.gov/2016047902

EDITORIAL CREDITS

Editor: Gena Chester
Designer: Veronica Scott
Media Researcher: Kelly Garvin
Production Specialist: Laura Manthe

04/18 B+T $27.99 JNF

PHOTO CREDITS

Capstopne Press/Karon Dubke, 17; Glow Images/Hero Images/Corbis, 24-25; iStockphoto: asiseelt, 29 (bottom), NicolasMcComber, 16; Shutterstock: Andrei_R, 9 (b), Andrey Burmakin, 29 (top), antoniodiaz, 27, Arina P Habich, 23, Cheryl Savan, 28, CREATISTA, 26, Creativa Images, 20, dragon_fang, 10 (b), Duplass, 5, ezheviks, 11, Fenf Yu, 9 (t), goodluz, 12, GooDween123, 10 (middle), hkeita, 8, jannoon028, 1 (right), Jelena Aloskina, 15, Lisa F. Young, 6, 21, mary981, 7 (b), NAN728, 10 (t), oksana2010, 18, Pepsco Studio, 22, Phovoir, 14, pogonici, 1, (left), ptnphoto, 19, Ruslan, cover, rvika, 2, 30, 32, STILLFX, 3, 31, ucchie79, 7 (t)

Artistic elements: Shutterstock: Art'nLera, grop, Marie Nimrichterova

Printed and bound in China.
004725

Table of Contents

Introduction
A Fantastic Business. 4

Chapter 1
Get Ready to Work 6

Chapter 2
Be the Best Babysitter 14

Chapter 3
Problem Solving. 18

Chapter 4
Your Next Steps 22

Glossary. 30
Read More. 31
Internet Sites 31
Index 32

INTRODUCTION
A FANTASTIC BUSINESS

If you like being around kids, babysitting is an awesome way to earn money. Parents often need babysitters in the evenings and on weekends, so it's the perfect job to fit in around school activities. Sitters are needed throughout the year, which means you can earn money all year long. And a babysitting business doesn't cost much to start or keep going.

With basic training and a few **marketing** materials, you'll be on your way to starting your small business. Your love of children and **professional** skills will assure your business grows into an amazing success. It's time to get started!

Tip

Get your parents' permission before starting a babysitting business. They may want to set limits on the number of hours or times of day that you work.

marketing—methods used by a company to convince people to buy its products or use its service

professional—demonstrating a generally businesslike manner in the home or workplace

No Experience? No Problem!

Do you think you'd like babysitting but haven't spent much time around young kids? A great way to gain experience is by volunteering. There may be community childcare programs in your area that need help. Or see if you can spend time with a neighbor's or relative's kids to help with childcare while the parent is home. Until you have enough experience, always make sure a trusted adult is nearby.

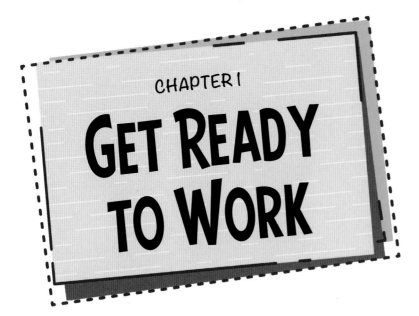

CHAPTER 1

GET READY TO WORK

The most successful businesses start with planning and preparation. Planning helps ensure that your babysitting service runs smoothly with minimal snags.

Take Classes

Before a parent hires you, they'll want to know you can keep their children safe. Training helps you feel more comfortable and confident as a sitter. National and local organizations offer babysitting courses that cover a variety of topics. Care of infants and children, handling emergencies, and dealing with behavior issues are some examples. **Cardiopulmonary resuscitation**, or CPR, training is important to have. Some courses also teach business basics. After successfully completing the course, students are given a certificate. They can show the certificate to possible **clients** and include it in a **resume**.

Tip

Health care groups and emergency-preparedness organizations, such as the Red Cross, offer CPR classes.

Know Your Limits

Taking care of a baby is very different from caring for an 8-year-old. Infants need more attention, while older children are more independent. Are you okay with changing diapers? What about feeding a baby? Or watching an energetic toddler? You'll need to decide if you want to limit your business to a certain age range. Also decide if you're comfortable caring for children with physical, developmental, or emotional special needs.

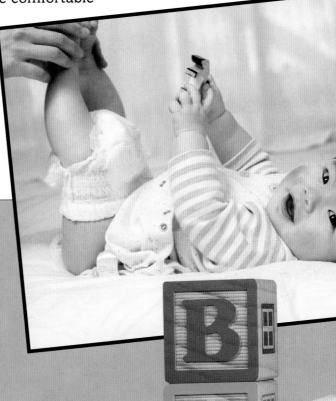

cardiopulmonary resuscitation—a method of restarting a heart that has stopped beating; CPR involves breathing into a patient's mouth and pressing on a patient's chest in a certain rhythm

client—a customer

resume—a brief listing of all the qualifications, skills, and experience a person has

Set a Price

Figuring out a fee can be tricky. You want to charge what you're worth. But asking for more money than other sitters in your area may keep parents from hiring you. In addition to the amount you want, decide how you want to be paid. Will your business be cash-only? Are checks okay? Do you expect to be paid at the end of every babysitting job? Whatever you choose, be very clear with your clients about what you expect.

Here are a few things to consider when deciding on a fee:

GOING RATE: Ask friends and family members who babysit in your area what they charge. Look at newspaper or online ads for babysitting services.

NUMBER OF KIDS: More kids mean more work, so a higher rate is okay. Have a base rate and increase it by a small amount for each additional child.

CHILDREN'S AGES: Babies need extra care and attention, so you can charge more for infants than older children.

SCHEDULED WORK: Does a parent need your help every Tuesday night from 6:00 to 9:00? Since the work is regular and guaranteed, you might consider charging a bit less.

Tip

Be realistic about what you can and can't handle. Scheduling jobs back to back without any free time can be overwhelming and stressful.

Finding Work

Now that you've taken classes and have decided on the scope of your business, it's time to find clients!

NETWORK: One of the best ways to find clients is by talking to people you know about your business. Tell friends, family, and neighbors about your new business. Networking is effective, easy, and free.

CLASSIFIED ADS: Announce your business to a wide range of people with a newspaper ad. If you can afford it, buy an ad in the services section. Most newspapers also have online versions of classified ads.

BABYSITTER REFERRALS: Sometimes other babysitters are so busy that they have to turn down work. In these cases, good babysitters keep a list of substitute sitters they can recommend to a client. Ask other sitters you know if they'll **refer** you to clients. Start a sitter referral list of your own in case you have to cancel.

CLIENT RECOMMENDATIONS: Once you've been working for a while, ask current clients to recommend you to other families. Just make sure those you ask are happy with the work you do!

refer—to recommend a person who might be of service

RESUME: A resume is a single page that lists your name and contact information at the top. It also summarizes your qualifications, skills, and experience. Be sure to include volunteer babysitting experience, especially if you're just starting out. Give your resume to families who may be interested in hiring you.

BUSINESS CARDS: Ask your parents if you can make and hand out business cards. Give them to parents you meet. Ask your parents, other family members, and friends to hand out cards for you. Business cards should include your name, type of business, and contact information.

Ken Adams
BABYSITTER
555-0998

FLYERS: A flyer is a larger handout that gives detailed information about you and your babysitting business. It contains some of the same information as a resume, but a flyer is more decorative and informal. You can leave flyers on your neighborhood doorsteps. But be cautious about where else you leave them in public. Never put your address on flyers.

BOOK A
BABYSITTER
FOR YOUR NEXT
DATE NIGHT!

Call now:
555-4512

template—a pattern used to make brochures, flyers, and business cards

Make Awesome Flyers

Business cards and flyers can be professionally printed or homemade. An online search of "babysitter flyers" will bring up lots of samples, including decorative *templates* that can be modified with your information. Here are some must-haves to include on a flyer:

• your name

• contact information

• hours you're available to babysit

• hourly pay rate

• a brief description about your training, experience, the services you provide, and what you like about kids and babysitting

Tip

Make sure you have your parents' permission before giving out any contact information.

BABYSITTING BUSINESS

CERTIFIED IN CPR
5 years experience with kids aged 2-13

$9.50 per hour
Available: weeknights 4:30 to 11 p.m.
weekends 8 a.m. to 11 p.m.
Call Liz at 555-3971

Interview the Family

It's tempting to take every job that comes along, especially when you're just starting a new business. But it's important to meet with the family and children before you decide to take them as clients. Come prepared to ask questions about the scope of your services.

During the interview, potential clients are deciding whether to hire you. So strive to make a good impression. Bring your resume, dress neatly, and arrive on time.

It's okay to decline a job if it's not a good fit. You need to feel confident that you can give the children the care they need. Politely tell the family your reasoning for not taking the job, and thank them for their time. Then try to recommend a sitter more suited to the family's needs.

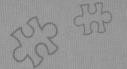

Make an Interview Questionnaire

Bring a questionnaire to a family interview. It's a great way to remember what to ask. During the interview, write down their answers to serve as a reminder of important details later on. Besides key contact information — such as family names, phone numbers, emergency numbers, and home address — ask about:

- number of children and their ages

- how the children like to spend their time

- day, time, and number of hours you'll be needed

- if you'll be expected to make meals, give baths, or do household chores

- food the kids can and can't eat

- house rules, such as how much TV time is allowed and bedtimes

- pets to look after

- transportation to and from the babysitting site (Never walk home alone at night, even if it's a short distance.)

Tip

When interviewing potential clients, stay safe by bringing a parent or trusted adult along. Do this especially if you've never met the client or the neighborhood is unfamiliar.

CHAPTER 2

BE THE BEST BABYSITTER

The goal of any successful business is to keep current clients happy and attract new ones. Here are some qualities that will help you achieve those goals.

BE DEPENDABLE: Arrive on time for every job. If you get sick or an emergency comes up, call the parents right away. If you can, make a referral to another good sitter.

BE RESPONSIBLE:

Play and interact with the kids in your care. Don't ignore them by texting, watching TV, or doing homework. Never invite friends over or eat the family's food without permission.

BE COURTEOUS: Speak politely. Respect the family and their home. Leave the house as clean or cleaner than when you arrived.

TAKE THE EXTRA STEP: Parents appreciate when sitters go the extra mile. If you have time, help kids with their homework or help them clean their room. But only do chores if you want to and if it doesn't interfere with watching the children.

PLAN AHEAD: Have some activities in mind to play with the children. Bring everything you think you'll need, such as games, puppets, drawing pads, and colored pencils. It's also a good idea to bring a first-aid kit.

BE PREPARED: Arrive 15 to 30 minutes early to your first job to get a tour of the house. Ask where items are located that you might need. Take notes to remember their instructions.

Fun Zone

Activities help keep children busy and happy. Engaged children are better behaved, which makes your job easier. First do some research and make sure an activity is a good fit for the children you're watching. Here are some activities children of different ages may enjoy. Remember: always get their parents' permission before doing any activity.

- **color or draw**
- **read aloud from a children's book**
- **watch an age-appropriate movie, such as a cartoon**
- **sing, make music, or dance**
- **take a walk around the neighborhood or go to a playground**
- **make a simple snack together, such as trail mix**

Musical Instruments

Most kids love making music. Add to the fun by playing instruments the children have created themselves. Make a drum from a turned-over plastic bin or metal can. A wooden spoon makes an ideal drumstick. Make a rattle by pouring dried beans into a glass or plastic jar and screwing on the lid.

Tip

Infants and toddlers can choke on small objects. Don't let children under the age of 3 play with any toy smaller than 1.3 inches (3.3 cm) in diameter. That's about the diameter of a Ping-Pong ball.

CHAPTER 3
PROBLEM SOLVING

With good planning and smart marketing, your babysitting service is hopefully off to a great start. But any business can hit unexpected snags. Watch for problems common to babysitting, and if they do happen, work to resolve them quickly.

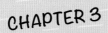

Tip

Put it in writing! Create a simple form that lists your pay rate and any other agreements you made with the family. Give the form to the parents before your first job.

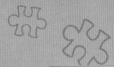

Payment Issues

Even though you made your payment terms clear, issues with payment can still arise. Sometimes a parent repeatedly doesn't have cash when they get home, and they ask if they can pay you next time. Other times the parents might pay you the wrong amount. Decide ahead of time how you'll handle these situations. Count cash when they hand it to you, or look at the check. If a parent has paid you less than your agreed-upon rate, it could be an oversight. Politely repeat your rate, and ask for the correct amount. If parents repeatedly ask to pay you next time, make it clear when you would like to be paid. Or inform them you won't be watching their children until they've paid you. Payment conversations can be difficult. The most important thing is to remain calm and confident.

Other Issues

Some situations make babysitting jobs unpleasant. For example:

- **A parent continually gets home later than agreed and doesn't call to let you know they'll be late.**
- **Dinner dishes fill the sink and a parent asks you to wash them.**
- **Parents give little to no notice for when they need your services. Or they call at inappropriate times of the day or night.**

What's the best solution? Calmly talk to the parents. Tell them exactly what's bothering you, why it's a problem, and how you'd like things to change. For example, if a parent keeps coming home late, you might say, "I know it's tough to get home exactly as planned, but I have other obligations that I need to meet. In the future, I hope you can get home at the time you promised."

Dropping a Client

If problems continue without any solution, it may be time to drop the family as a client. Politely but firmly tell the parents you can no longer babysit for them. You can recommend another sitter to the family, as long as that sitter is aware of the potential problems. Tell the family how much you have appreciated their business. Leave on good terms to help ensure your business keeps a good reputation.

CHAPTER 4
YOUR NEXT STEPS

Successful business owners evaluate their businesses from time to time. After several months, think about your babysitting business. Are you ready for more clients? Are you making money but not saving enough? A few additional steps will help to ensure you get the results you want.

It pays to be trustworthy and reliable! A 2012 survey by American Red Cross found that more than half of parents needing a babysitter canceled their plans because they couldn't find reliable help.

Grow Your Business

If you're ready for more work, there are many ways to grow your business. But make sure you don't exceed your limit. Otherwise you could easily become overwhelmed. Here are a few suggestions for finding new clients:

- **Branch out into new neighborhoods and/or different age groups.**
- **Increase the days and hours you work.**
- **Remind relatives, friends, and neighbors about your business and keep business cards and flyers handy.**
- **Create a new flyer that reflects your increased level of experience, new rates, and any other changes to your business. Include that references are available upon request if you have families who have agreed to serve as references for you. Update your resume with new work experience and references.**

References

References are a great marketing tool. They are given by people who have hired you in the past who are willing to make positive statements about your work. A reference can be in the form of a letter that you can copy and give to potential clients. Or a parent might allow you to share their phone number or email address so a possible client can contact them directly.

reference—a person who can make statements about a job seeker's character and abilities

Ask for a Raise

After you've worked with a client for a year or more, it's appropriate to ask for a raise. First, tell the parents you'd like to set a time to talk about a business matter. Try to meet in a place where the children are not around. Explain that you'd like a raise, and then list your skills and the things you've accomplished for the family. If they don't agree to a raise right away, ask what more you can do to deserve one. See if they'll consider a raise in six months.

Tip

Talking firmly to an adult can be tough! Remind yourself that this is a business and it's your responsibility to make it successful. Be polite, but speak with confidence.

Babysitter Burnout

Is it possible to be too successful? Absolutely. You have a busy life with school, friends, and activities. Being too busy is not good for you or the children you care for. If babysitting becomes too stressful, it might be time to cut back on jobs. Politely drop as many clients as necessary. Explain to the family that you're cutting back to meet personal needs. Emphasize that you really care for the family and that they've done

nothing wrong to upset you. Try to recommend a reliable sitter to take your place. Be aware that the family may try to talk you into changing your mind, so you'll need to state your wishes firmly. You can always tell the family this is temporary if you think you'll be less stressed in the future.

Are you feeling burned out because you've lost the joy of babysitting? See if you can make it fun again. Try focusing on the aspects of childcare you really enjoy. You could limit your service to the age range you prefer, such infants rather than older children. Taking a break from paid babysitting might also help. Instead read to children at the library, coach a sports team, or tutor at school.

Manage Your Money

Making money is awesome, but it also comes with responsibility. Do you spend or save? Some money experts say it's best to do both — spend a little and save a little.

It's easy to spend too much, so deciding between wants and needs is one way to limit spending. A "want" is something that you can live without. A "need" is something that's necessary for daily life. For example, you need clothes to wear. But do you really need that expensive pair of designer shoes?

If clients pay with checks, you'll need to open a bank account. Banks keep money safe, and the lack of easy access will cut down on the temptation to spend. Ask your parents for help if you haven't already opened an account.

Tip

Set aside a certain percentage of money each time you get paid. Try saving at least 20 percent. You'll be surprised how quickly it adds up!

Once you start your babysitting business, you'll see that caring for kids is fun and rewarding. It's a fantastic business that's as flexible as you need it to be.

GLOSSARY

cardiopulmonary resuscitation (kahr-dee-oh-PUHL-muh-nayr-ee ree-suh-suh-TAY-shuhn)—a method of restarting a heart that has stopped beating; CPR involves breathing into a patient's mouth and pressing on a patient's chest in a certain rhythm

client (KLY-uhnt)—a customer

marketing (MAR-ke-ting)—methods used by a company to convince people to buy its products or use its service

professional (pruh-FEH-shuh-nuhl)— demonstrating a generally businesslike manner in the home or workplace

reference (REF-uh-renss)—a person who can make statements about a job seeker's character and abilities

referral (ri-FUR)—to recommend a person who might be of service

resume (RE-zuh-may)—a brief listing of all the qualifications, skills, and experience a person has

template (TEM-plate)—a pattern used to make brochures, flyers, and business cards

READ MORE

Berne, Emma Carlson. *Run Your Own Babysitting Business.* Young Entrepreneurs. New York: PowerKids Press, 2014.

Brown, Harriet. *Babysitting: The Care and Keeping of Kids.* A Smart Girl's Guide. Middleton, Wis.: American Girl Publishing, 2014.

Colich, Abby. *A Babysitter's Guide to Keeping the Kids Entertained.* Go-To Guides. North Mankato, Minn.: Capstone Press, 2017.

INTERNET SITES

FactHound offers a safe, fun way to find Internet sites related to this book. All of the sites on FactHound have been researched by our staff.

Here's all you do:
Visit *www.facthound.com*

Type in this code: 9781515766919

 Check out projects, games and lots more at
www.capstonekids.com

INDEX

activities, 15, 16–17, 26

ads, 8, 9

burnout, 26–27

business cards, 10, 11, 23

flyers, 10–11, 23

interview, 12–13

marketing, 4, 18

networking, 9

pay, 8, 11, 19
  raise, 25

problems, 18–19, 20, 21

references, 23

referrals, 9, 14

resume, 6, 10, 12, 23

skills, 4, 10

spending, 28

training, 4, 6, 11

volunteering, 5, 10